THE LOTUS ESPRIT

MATT YOUNGER
AND MIKE YOUNGER

AMBERLEY

First published 2017

Amberley Publishing
The Hill, Stroud,
Gloucestershire, GL5 4EP

www.amberley-books.com

Map illustration by Thomas Bohm, User Design, Illustration and Typesetting.

ISBN: 978 1 4456 6983 0 (print)
ISBN: 978 1 4456 6984 7 (ebook)

British Library Cataloguing in Publication Data.
A catalogue record for this book is available from the British Library.

Typeset in 10pt on 13pt Celeste.
Typesetting by Amberley Publishing.
Printed in the UK.

Appointed GPSR EU Representative: Easy Access System Europe Oü, 16879218
Address: Mustamäe tee 50, 10621, Tallinn, Estonia
Contact Details: gpsr.requests@easproject.com, +358 40 500 3575

Contents

Acknowledgements

We would like to thank the following people for their contributions of photographs of their beautiful Esprits: Paul Clapham (Yellow Esprit S1), Jonathon Hackford (White Esprit S1), Andrew Weaver (Black Stevens), Mark Blanchard (Red Stevens), Dean (West Sussex – JPS S2), Jim Richardson (JPS Interior), Andy Warne (White Guigiaro with Concorde), David Murray-Hundley (V8 Sport 350), Stuart Monument (Active Esprit photos), Barrie Comes (Essex Esprit Turbo).

Special thanks to Group Lotus for their contribution of photos of unique Esprits across the years – grateful thanks!

Thank you to everyone who sent photos, even if we couldn't use all of them. We will put the rest on our website – www.lotusclubonline.co.uk

Thanks also to Stuart Monument for his article about his Active Esprit.

We would like to dedicate this book to two special individuals who are no longer with us; Roger Becker, forty-three years at Lotus Cars – famously driving the Esprit for Bond in *The Spy Who Loved Me* – who died during the writing of this book, and our father, Bob, who isn't around to see us in print. RIP gentlemen!

1

Lotus Forever

It was a day like any other. I was on an errand for my dear mother, to the local shop. I rounded the corner onto the area in front of the shop and there it was! I stopped in my tracks at the sight of a black and gold sports car that was so low I was amazed. It was the rear I saw first; a flat deck with purposeful grills on either side and through the tiny rear window I could see more dials than I had ever seen in a car before. I spent ages walking around it and gazing in the windows at the interior. The reclining black sports seats had me captivated and the low nose with the yellow and green badge and the gold coachlines finished off the vision that was the Lotus Europa – a JPS celebration model at that. That was my first sight of a real Lotus; the shop owner's JPS Europa. I went on many more errands after that, without any coercion, always hoping to see the Europa parked somewhere near the shop.

A Lotus Europa in JPS colours.

A little later, just after starting secondary school, a friend gave me a copy of *Speed & Power* magazine that had an article about a car based on a truck chassis that looked like a Ford Capri on steroids and had a Rolls-Royce Merlin engine crushed into the front! It was awesome, but temperamental. It wasn't this article that took my eye and forced me to the newsagent to get my own copy, though – it was the article entitled 'A Lotus for the Elite'. There were pictures and a cutaway drawing of the new Lotus Elite and I was in love. Again! My family didn't even own a car at the time and the only car owners locally had Vauxhall Vivas and Ford Escort mark 1s with the odd mark 2. The Lotus was a shock to the senses with its wedge shape and beautifully sloping bonnet, pop-up headlamps and seriously alluring, cutting-edge wheels. I even wrote to Lotus Cars to request a brochure! My dad thought I was as daft as a brush – especially when I told him the price! He said I could buy a house for that sort of money. I started wondering, how could I live in an Elite? It had a cigar lighter socket, so making coffee would't be a problem. I vowed then that I would own a Lotus before I was thirty.

I kept up with my reading as the Eclat and then the Esprit were released. I read every road test in detail, several hundred times over. The articles ended up on my wall beside my bed. One thing I never could understand was, why when the Lotus Esprit Turbo hammered the Ferrari 308 in every part of *Car Magazine*'s test, they still came down on the side of the Ferrari? In true car journalist fashion, the badge turning every article into a re-telling of the Emperor's New Clothes for car lovers! Now in my mature years I understand more of the designer label, junket culture and it all makes a lot more sense – a trip to Norfolk not being half as interesting as one to Italy.

The fact is that the Lotus Esprit is one of the most striking pieces of automotive design to emerge from this country, or any other. Its amazing twenty-seven-year production run is testament to its unique heritage and desirability and its development throughout this time undoubtably kept Lotus in the business of making road cars. As you will find as you read on, there have been twenty-three variations of the Esprit produced, starting with a 2-litre normally aspirated 155 bhp 4-cylinder engine and ending with a 3.5 litre, twin turbocharged V8 with 350 bhp available. There was one major, and countless minor, styling changes over the years – the major one being the re-design of the Esprit by Peter Stevens in 1987. With all of these models and specifications to choose from, prospective owners

The original Esprit S1.

usually have a model in mind, or are bewildered to start with. This book should help you to hone in on the Esprit that most suits your desires, and your pocket.

The thing is that Lotuses of a certain period are not complicated or difficult to understand or dismantle; the average mechanic can deal with everything that you are likely to need done, but this is heresy in this day of paying for the privilege of ownership of a design icon and paying for the badge.

So how does all of this help with your idea or yearning for ownership? Well, this book should not only show you what a unique and brilliant car the Lotus Esprit actually is, but also how you can realise your dream of ownership without actually selling your soul to do so.

Driving the Esprit

My very first drive of an Esprit was of an Esprit S2 in the early nineties. I had worked my way up from the family Austin Maxi through my own fast Fords and was the proud owner of an XR3i (although I much preferred my XR3!) when Mike showed up one day with his S2 and offered me a drive.

First impressions were of how absolutely beautiful it was. The Speedline wheels and slight body improvements on the S1 really made the Esprit look Italian and emphasised its supercar claims. It was a bronze colour and the interior was a collection of browns and beiges, looking like a design prototype rather than a road car. I snatched the chance of a drive – it might be the only chance I ever got to drive an Esprit. I had waited for this moment since reading about the S1 in 1976!

My climb into the cabin was neither easy nor graceful. I am six foot four inches tall and I managed to snag my knees on the wheel, my head on the roof, and my jeans on the handbrake in the door sill – standard enough for an Esprit virgin then! Once in I found it extremely strange; the windscreen plunges away from you into the distance, and everything else seems to be almost at shoulder height. Your backside feels like it is scraping the road and when the door closes you are firmly cosseted in the otherwise very comfortable seat. All of the controls are easily reached and simple to use, but they make you feel like you are in a jet fighter when you are used to lesser transport.

Mike's Esprit S2.

The starter always sounds a bit tinny on the 4-cylinder models, but the engine sounds meaty and purposeful when it starts, rather than just 'loud' like modern hot hatches. Then I find that my feet are rather large for the Esprit as well. My size 11s need light training shoes to drive an Esprit with confidence – certainly nothing with oversized soles as the pedals are fit for a ballerina!

Once it is moving, you find the steering feels heavy to start with but as you reach walking speed it lightens up and as you reach normal road speeds it becomes absolutely perfect. It is delicate, direct and confidence-building. You find you can feel the road – every change of camber or grip – and your faith in the handling and road-holding of the Esprit grows in proportion to the grin on your face.

It's so like a go-kart. Some of this impression comes from sitting so close to the road with your feet beside the front wheel. You feel like you are literally connected to the front wheels by telepathy. A flex of the wrists is enough to guide the Esprit through most bends and you can feel that it knew where to go without your conscious input.

The original normally aspirated Esprits are not what would be described as 'fast' cars. With 0 to 60 mph in around 6.7 seconds, a modern up-market coupe or 'sports' saloon would be able to boast the same figures, but the comparison ends there. To drive quickly in the Esprit (who would dare to mention fast these days?) you get into a rhythm and feel your way from bend to bend like you are part of the car. You won't need to slow your progress for bends, just feel your way through the twisty bits and keep powering on. No computer interference – none required – as you enjoy one of the best sports cars ever built. It really is all about 'feel'. The Esprit feels wonderful, like you are 'plugged in' to the car and you tell it how you want to proceed and it tells you all about the road and the grip available. Try finding a review of a contemporary sports car that could touch the Esprit in this area.

I have since driven Esprit Turbos, Turbo SEs and the V8 Esprit, and all shared the original's connection between driver and the road whilst adding speed and stopping power with a vengeance! My last drive of the V8 was a revelation. So unbelievably quiet and immensely quick, with brakes that knocked the air out of my lungs when my expectations were massively exceeded coming up to a tight left-hander!

Mike's Esprit S2 Interior.

2

Model History & Specifications

Model History

The Esprit has arguably one of the longest model histories of any modern day sports car, with the possible exception of the Porsche 911. It is again an arguable point that there is little shared by the early 911s and those on sale today. Indeed, Porsche itself assigns a different number to its newer models as it produces a variant. The Esprit, however, has retained much of its underpinnings and dimensions throughout its twenty-seven-year development history. Though engines, suspension, brakes and much more have changed and evolved throughout the years, the Esprit retained its initial characteristics and its presence on the road throughout.

There are many excellent publications that detail the history and detail changes to the Esprit over the years. However, we couldn't write a book for prospective owners of an Esprit without giving a brief, if less complete, guide to how the Esprit has changed from model to model through the years, to better inform your choice.

In 1970, Tony Rudd recommended two new Lotus models; the M50 Elite front-engined models to take over from the Elan +2S, and the M70 mid-engined models to take over from the Europa. Lotus resources, however, were still quite stretched. Management decided to concentrate on the Type 907 engine and the development of the front-engined cars, so development of the mid-engined Esprit was still to come.

In the autumn of 1971, Mike Kimberly was given the job of transforming the Europa. The Europa was never considered a stylishly attractive car and was not equipped with a spacious cockpit. The M70 would have to be more practical and stylish than this. The styling of the new car got under way in 1971, following a meeting between Colin Chapman and Giorgetto Giugiaro of Ital Design. Giugiaro wanted to design a new body style for the Lotus. Chapman, with the M70 in mind, agreed to let him work on the basis of a mid-engined Europa.

The very first Giugiaro styling for Lotus was based on the much-modified Europa Twin-Cam chassis. He was also working on the Maserati Boomerang project at the time. The Type 907 engine was soon to be installed and the track and wheelbase dimensions were to be altered. The Europa wheelbase was 7 foot 7 inches and its widest track was

4 foot 5.5 inches. The M70 wheelbase was 8 foot and 4 foot 11.5 inches for track. The chassis supplied to Italy was thus lengthened and widened. This, however, was not Lotus' final word on the subject.

Work began on the style in mid-1971 and was completed by the end of that year as a full size mock up. In 1972 a more advanced and integrated design of the chassis was completed, painted silver and logically known as 'the silver car'! It made its debut on the Ital Design stand at the Turin Motor Show of November 1972. Giugiaro had dubbed it the 'Esprit' and it stood alongside the Maserati Boomerang project at that show.

Lotus' reaction to the completed prototype was so favourable, as Mike Kimberley recalls, that a development team was immediately set up to work with Giugiaro and stayed in Italy for at least eighteen months. Chapman and Kimberley flew to Turin twice a week, during which the body style was refined and turned into a production-possible proposition. There was a lull after the public showing of 1972 while mechanical design work got underway.

In 1974 the first true production prototype was nearly completed by Christmas and was used to pick up Colin Chapman from Heathrow airport in January 1975 on his return from the Argentine Grand Prix. Lotus then confirmed that the Esprit would be launched during 1975.

To provide more passenger space and to accommodate the more bulky Type 907 engine, the wheelbase of the M70 was to be 8 foot – or 5 inches longer than that of the Europa. The engine would be rated at 160 bhp (DIN) with the cylinder block leaning at 45 degrees to the left side of the chassis.

Right from the start Lotus' biggest problem was to find a suitable gearbox, which was critical to the entire project. This was to remain a problem, even at the end of its model run. The Type 907 produced 140 lb/foot of torque, even in 2-litre form. The highest of the Lotus-Ford twin-cam had been 113 lb/foot of torque. The Renault 5-speed as used in the Europa would not be strong enough for the job. Lotus could not afford to design their own gearbox as the cost would be immense, so they had to look around, in true Lotus style, for an off-the-shelf transaxle.

The 'Silver Car' concept for the Esprit. Courtesy of Lotus Cars.

Lotus could go shopping almost anywhere for a transaxle. They, however, were looking for a 5-speed transmission with ample reserves of strength and which had mechanical 'elegance' that was light and would be guaranteed supply for many years to come. The search began in 1971 and the first Citroen production units were not fitted until 1975–76, and were still being used in the mid-1980s.

The search ended when Citroen offered Lotus the use of their 5-speed all-synchromesh gearbox/final-drive unit, which was being used in the front-engine/front-drive SM coupe and the mid-engine/rear-drive Maserati Merak coupe (but not the Merak SS). Even though the SM is now long dead and the Merak ceased production in the early 1980s, Lotus still have no supply problems from France.

Lotus had to look at the gearbox again for the V8 engine project which produced a great deal more torque than the 2-litre 'four' and again the gearbox would not be capable of transmitting this level of power reliably.

With the backbone frame chosen and the engine and transmission finalized and the front suspension basically that of the Opel Ascona/Vauxhall Cavalier, the rest of the mechanics fitted into place. The steering was rack and pinion without power assistance; no Esprit or Turbo needed this. The brakes were dual circuit Girling brakes – front and rear discs but not ventilated – with the rear discs mounted inboard. The system was not servo assisted. The wheels were cast-alloy 14-inch diameter Wolfrace, with 7-inch rims at the rear and 6-inch at the front.

The shape was designed to make it cheaper to build in quantity. The angle of the windscreen had to be changed to meet regulations as the original on the 'Silver' prototype had been angled at 19 degrees from horizontal. It had to be raised to 24 degrees 5 minutes. There was more space for passengers but not for luggage – the seats were steeply reclined, as in the Europa.

The Esprit was not ready for production when it was announced to be. In October 1975, Lotus thought it necessary to reveal the car at the same time as the Eclat, which was ready at that time. Lotus' reasoning was that the car had been known to the public for three years already and customers might despair that it would never be announced if not shown then.

For several reasons, Lotus forecast losses in profit for 1975, which meant the Esprit was delayed by nine months due to financial pressures.

In May 1976 the first series production car was commissioned and deliveries began in June and July.

The Esprit S1

In October 1975 the Esprit's UK price was fixed at £5,844 (the Elite 501 was £6,493) but by the time deliveries began in the summer of 1976, it had rocketed to £7,833; a 35 per cent increase. The published price in October 1975 was not realistic as the company cost accountants had to make huge adjustments in a matter of a few months. Lotus' hopes of producing a more up-market replacement for the Europa could have been adversely affected on the issue of price.

The first Esprits were disappointing; they were not as fast or refined as Lotus had hoped. The up-market vision looked to be tarnished. Lotus built 70 per cent of the car and the

The Esprit S1 of 1976.

The original Esprit S1 interior in alcantara and tartan cloth.

rest was made up of Citroen parts – the gearbox, wheels (Wolfrace) and tyres, electrical equipment and springs and dampers.

Lotus claimed the original Esprit could reach 138 mph but independent tests, as done by *Autocar*, found it only reached 124 mph, and *Motor* could only achieve a figure of just over 125 mph. The lack of refinement was more of a problem; after more than three years of development the problems of excessive engine noise in the cockpit and overall harshness were evident. However, its handling and road performance along with its good looks were evidently its selling points. Once again, Lotus' handling was paramount.

In 1977 the Esprit was intended for the states. Peter Pulver, Lotus' main Stateside distributor, ordered 150 at the Earls Court Show in 1976 and deliveries began in 1977. The Type 907 engine with its U.S. market Zenith-Stromberg carburettors passed the emission-reduction tests with flying colours – so much so that the net power output was still 140 bhp so the car had a top speed of 120 mph in fourth or fifth gears. The east coast price was $15,990 or $16,844 in California.

The US launch had a dramatic effect on Esprit production, which had been 138 in 1976 and now went up to 580 in 1977. Only 4 cars were built for the UK in 1976 but in 1977, 474 were built for the USA.

The Esprit S2

In August 1978 the S2 model was launched. After adverse press comments and criticism, Lotus made speedy attempts to improve the S1. As the inflation rate was still high, the price of the Esprit rocketed. At launch the S2 was priced at £11,124; 9 per cent higher than the last of the S1s, though it was a much improved package. It had standardised 'E-Camshaft' specification and Speedline road wheels replaced the Wolfrace brand.

Above: The Esprit S2 of 1978.

Right: Speedline wheels – so Italian!

The Lotus publicity picture taken at Hethel, courtesy of Lotus Cars.

There were improvements to the style externally. The front spoiler was now more smoothly integrated into the shape of the car, spoiler intakes were neatly placed behind the rear quarter windows, and Rover SD1-type tail lamp clusters were fitted.

There was an interesting innovation made to cut costs and minimise space in the front bonnet compartment. The spare wheel was reduced to a 5.5-inch-wide rim and carried a small 185/70 HR 13-inch tyre, used merely as a 'get home' tyre not for prolonged use after a puncture.

Lotus launched a special 'limited edition' Esprit S2 at the first NEC Motor Show in October 1978, decked out in black and gold to commemorate Mario Andretti winning the Formula 1 World Championship in the Lotus 79.

Each car was individually numbered by a plaque on the dashboard and signed by Colin Chapman. There were supposed to be 147 of these 'JPS' models built but numbers of actual cars produced were much less.

S2 performance in *Autocar's* press car was 130 mph, with 0 to 60 mph achieved in 8.0 seconds. The drag coefficient of 0.34 was virtually unaffected by the changes to the bodywork. Overall it was a step in the right direction for refinement and reliability and the launch of the Chrysler Sunbeam-Lotus in March 1979 seemed to prove that. 1,061 S2s were built.

The Esprit S2 with new rear lights.

The Esprit S2 new interior, steering wheel and trim.

Above: Updated instrument binnacle.

Left: A Lotus publicity shot of the S2 JPS limited edition. Courtesy of Lotus Cars.

The JPS Esprit limited edition wearing the F1 team colours.

Esprit JPS interior trim.

The JPS edition is still striking today.

An Esprit S2.2, looking exactly like the S2.

In 1980 and 1981, Lotus produced a very limited run of approximately 49 cars named the S2.2. This car featured the new, larger 2.2-litre version of the 907 engine, designated the 912. The car also had a galvanised chassis. There were very few other changes other than superficial.

1980: The Esprit Turbo

The launch of the Esprit Turbo in 1980 featured the new 910 engine with a dry sump and 2.2 litres. The first cars were painted in the livery of Essex petroleum, who were sponsoring the F1 team at the time.

An Esprit Turbo in 'Essex' livery.

Lotus's shot of the Essex Turbo at Hethel.

Note the Compomotive wheels, Rover SD1 rear lights, and NACA ducts in the sill.

Though the car still carries the Esprit tag, the 1980 Turbo Esprit was effectively a new car, where the 16-valve engine has been enlarged to 2,174 cc, using a bore of 95.25 mm, and a stroke of 76.20 mm. The 4-cylinder aluminium engine provides, Lotus claimed, 210 bhp at 6,250 rpm and 200 lb/foot of torque at 4,500 rpm. A Garrett T3 turbocharger, which is mounted before the twin Dellorto DHLA carburettors (modified to take the boosted induction), supplies boost up to 8 lb psi, and the engine operates on a 7.5:1 compression ratio. The turbocharger lubrication is direct from the main oil gallery, with oil drain to the dry sump (which later changed to a wet sump). The inlet manifold was shortened to reduce turbo lag and the turbo situated as close to the exhaust manifold as possible.

The gearbox remained the same but the chassis was changed and improved. It became galvanised and warranted for five years. The front section was widened and new suspension pick-up points were used. Torsional stiffness was increased and larger radiators allowed. The front suspension was borrowed from the Elite but had a wider track.

The original dry sump turbo engine.

Contrasting, sumptuous interior trim.

Left: Optional roof console stereo!

Below: Johnny Herbert behind the wheel!

The Esprit Turbo, a massive step up for the Esprit!

The Esprit Turbo's louvered tailgate to allow for greater cooling.

Bodywork and interior were changed extensively, the main differences being a louvered tailgate allowing cooling of the engine compartment, larger wrap-around front spoiler, NACA ducts in the sills, a larger rear lip spoiler, BBS alloy wheels, and an interior sporting a boost gauge for the turbo and central air-conditioning controls. Performance was devastating at 0–60 mph in 5.5 seconds (claimed) and a 150 mph top speed together with a 23 mpg figure.

Specifications:

Model Year: (1980)
Engine: Lotus Type 910 2,174 cc Garrett AiResearch turbo charged
Power: 210 bhp @ 6250 rpm
Torque: 200 lb/foot @ 4,250 rpm
Gearbox: Maserati SM 5-speed
Chassis: Steel backbone with two prongs at the rear and tubular structure
Front suspension: Double wishbones and coil spring/damper units
Rear suspension: Wide-based lower wishbones, upper transverse links and coil spring/damper units
Brakes: 10.5 inch discs front – 9.7 inch inboard discs rear
Wheelbase: 8 feet 0 inches
Front Track: 4 feet 11.5 inches
Rear Track: 5 feet 0.5 inches
Overall Length: 13 feet 9 inches
Width: 6 feet 1.25 inches
Weight: 1,060 kg

It trounced the Ferrari 308 GTB in every area – a fact referred to by Mike Kimberley himself – but still *Car* magazine patronised the Italians when the two were tested together. I know which of the two cars I would have bought then, and indeed now!

There were supposed to be forty-five Essex Turbos built, but we cannot verify this figure.

Looking good in silver and showing off the new front spoiler and ducts.

The Esprit S3

In 1981 the S3 was launched. This was a sensible and shrewd move by Lotus. The S3 took the Turbo chassis and used the 912 engine at 2.2 litres to produce the best normally aspirated Esprit so far. Suspension characteristics were tailored to the performance of the car and the interior was brought up to Esprit Turbo standards (minus the boost gauge of course!).

A total of 767 S3s were sold between 1981 and 1987. The body got the turbo bumpers and front spoiler, with colour coding all round. The sills did not have the NACA ducts and the tailgate did not require the louvers of the turbo but the BBS alloys and Goodyear NCT tyres were retained. The car was also given 50% more soundproofing effect. 0–60 mph came up in 6.5 seconds with 160 bhp available at 6,500 rpm and 160 lb/foot of torque at the same.

A brace of S3s and a turbo relative in the background.

Esprit S3, elegant and sporting.

An early Esprit Turbo engine bay with the turbo at the far right.

From 1981 to 1986 the Esprit Turbo was built. Lotus continued to develop the Esprit Turbo throughout this period. The dry sump configuration was changed to a normal wet sump system, problems with checking the oil level in the dry sump models being one reason for the change.

The Esprit Turbo HC

In 1987 the Turbo HC was launched. Lotus re-worked the turbo engine extensively to redress criticisms of its delivery. Lessons learnt on the Excel were used around the intake areas and larger Dellorto carburettor fitted (DHLA45Ms). These had a balance pipe as on the Excel, though this had to be reinforced to deal with the pressurisation from the turbo.

The HC tag comes from the higher compression ratio, raised to 8:1, a decent rise when added to extra boost from the modified Garrett T3 turbo charger. This went up to 9.5 psi. The peak power went up 5 bhp to 215 bhp and more importantly the torque figure rose to 220 lb/foot at a more useable 4,250 rpm. Mid-range punch was increased substantially. Bodywork stayed the same with different decals and the interior was improved with adjustable seat backs and a remote tailgate release.

Specifications: (1976–2004)

Engine: Lotus Type 910

Max power: 215 bhp (PS-DIN) (160 kW ISO) at 6,250 rpm. Max torque: 2,201 lb/foot (298 Nm) at 4,250 rpm

The Esprit Turbo HC with side decals proclaiming the changes.

The HC leather interior.

New decals to distinguish the HC Turbo from the previous model.

The HC Turbo engine with improvements and red cam covers.

The much improved HC Turbo.

Chassis: Steel backbone with two prongs at the rear and tubular structure
Front Suspension: independent, double wishbone. Coil springs, telescopic dampers, and-roll bar
Rear Suspension: Independent, upper and lower transverse link with radius arms, coil springs, telescopic dampers, anti-roll bar
Brakes: Front 10.1 inch (258 mm) diameter ventilated discs. Rear 10.8 inch (275.9mm) diameter discs
Overall dimensions unchanged
Weight: 1,148 kg

1987–90: The Peter Steven Esprit (Normally Aspirated and Turbo)

The type code for the new face-lifted car was X180 and it was launched in October 1987, with cars being sold almost immediately. Peter Stevens gently rounded the traditional Esprit lines and the result was very beautiful. The tailgate received a glass panel, almost Italian, which was able to allow air from the engine compartment to escape and the owner to view the engine.

Wheels were from Route OZ. The gearbox/transaxle was changed to that from the Renault GTA, giving a higher 3.88:1 final drive. Brakes were placed in the conventional outboard situation and were solid discs at the rear and ventilated at the front. Little had changed in the engine specification.

The interior was reworked to great effect. There was improved cabin space and a new instrument binnacle. The car feels less claustrophobic than the original Esprit and the face lift gave the Esprit a new lease of life.

The normally aspirated Esprit was continued with exactly the same performance statistics as the S3 it replaced: 172 bhp at 6,500 rpm and 160 lb/foot torque – 0–60 in 6.5 seconds. It was only produced between 1988 and 1990 and was the last of the normally aspirated Esprits.

The new-look Esprit Turbo at Hethel, Lotus Cars publicity picture.

The Stevens Esprit Turbo.

The new rear with glass panel.

Reworked and roomier interior.

Stunning in black with a nod to Bond!

Specifications: (1987)

Engine: Lotus type 910

Max power 215 bhp (PS-DIN) (160 kW ISO) at 6,000 rpm. Max torque 2,201 lb/foot (298 Nm) at 4,250 rpm

Chassis: Steel backbone with two prongs at the rear and tubular structure

Front Suspension: Independent, double wishbone. Coil springs, telescopic dampers, and-roll bar

Rear Suspension: Independent, upper and lower transverse link with radius arms, coil springs, telescopic dampers, anti-roll bar

Brakes: Front 10.1 inch (258 mm) diameter ventilated discs. Rear 10.8 inch (275.9 mm) diameter discs

Weight: 3,250 lb (1,386 kg)

1989–92: The Turbo SE

The SE model was introduced in May 1989. This model received charge-cooling; boosting power to 264 bhp and improving the 0–60 figure to 4.7 seconds. The engine also gained fuzzy-logic engine management and fuel injection at this point. The model was so well received that Lotus sold 563 cars in its first year alone. 1,600 were produced until 1994 when it was replaced by the S4. Luxury fittings were added to the interior, with walnut burr facia (Elm burr actually) and additions of a lift-out roof panel, air-conditioning, and ice-warning light. After October 1990, anti-lock brakes became an option for the first time.

What you see from the driving seat in the SE.

The interior of limited edition Esprit SE.

The Esprit S

This model was also produced during this period, being the turbo version of the SE without charge-cooling. The power was raised to 228 bhp using the fuel injection system and engine management of the SE. Getting from 0–60 mph was achieved in 5.2 secs.

The Esprit Turbo

The Esprit Turbo was also produced, having the carburettor engine of the older cars (this had the older glass tailgate.) There are very few examples of the S around (this had the previous turbo's tailgate). All three models had the SE chassis and settings but bodywork was based on older models in the S and Turbo while Lotus used up spare materials, running the production of these models down.

In 1991–92 the racing X180R was also produced. This was not a road car – it was an Esprit racer.

The X180R in action. An out and out racer! Picture courtesy of Lotus Cars.

1992–1993: The Esprit SE High Wing

This model spanned the gap to the introduction of the S4 with its distinctively outrageous rear wing. There were little changes of note other than to aerodynamic details and the interior.

1993–96: The S4

This retained the engine specification from the SE. It was a styling exercise to stimulate interest in the Esprit that produced a very distinctive car with body changes to the front spoiler, sills, and an extra wing mounted mid-way up the tailgate.

The ancient Morris Marina door handles went, at last, to be replaced by those from the Rover 200. New 5-spoke wheels were added and power-assisted steering was provided for the first time ever. A new Nardi steering wheel, GM switchgear, and carbon-fibre trim replaced the previous interior appointments.

The S4 Esprit with new wheels, spoilers and detail changes.

Showing off its new wheels and impressive rear spoiler. Picture courtesy of Lotus Cars.

Wheel arch extensions made the overall impression much more impressive, and there were suspension tweaks and a changed anti-roll bar and springs and dampers on the front, as well as new castings for the engine, block, head and sump were changed and stiffened. The engine was remapped to deliver better torque at low revs and a strengthened Renault gearbox was needed. Ten days after the S4 was launched, Lotus Cars was put up for sale!

1995: Esprit S4S

The model that slotted between the S4 and the Sport 300 (the S4S boasts the same 300 bhp of the Sport 300). It was to have the driving qualities of the Sport 300 and the ride and detailing of the S4 and was a big success.

The S4s – the top of the 4-cylinder tree!

This particular S4 has the wheels used on the V8, rather than the split-rim OZ items fitted to the standard car.

The reworked and more powerful engine.

The extra performance stemmed from improved gas flow dynamics and enlarged inlet ports and valves are the main cylinder head modifications. A hybrid Garrett AiResearch T3/60 turbocharger and altered management programme give the engine even more torque over a wider spread. Of the 290 lb/foot maximum, 80 per cent is available anywhere between 2,500 and 6,500 rpm.

Specifications:

Engine: Turbocharger: Garrett T3 .63 with 0.60 Compressor, water-cooled with integral wastegatePower: 300 bhp / 7,000 rpm Torque: 290 lb/foot / 3,600 rpm
Gearbox: Type: five-speed manual, rear-wheel drive
Suspension: Front – Independent via double wishbones, coil springs, anti-roll bar Rear – Independent via transverse links and radius arms, coil springs
Wheels: OZ Racing light alloy, 8.5J x 17 front, 10Jx18 rear
Tyres: Michelin Pilot MXX3, 235/40 ZR17 front, 285/35 ZR18 rear
Brakes: Front/rear: ventilated discs, ABS
Steering: Type: rack and pinion, power assisted

Dimensions:
Wheelbase: 2,420 mm
Overall length: 4,414 mm
Overall width: 1,883 mm
Overall height: 1,150 mm
Kerb weight: 1,460 kg
Dry Weight: 1,325kg

Performance:
0–60 mph: 4.6 seconds
0–100 mph: 11.4 seconds
Maximum speed: 168 mph

The S4S has the 300's rear wing and wheel arch extensions and also has distinctive OZ split rim racing alloy with 245 and 285 section Michelin pilot tyres. Big ventilated discs and callipers are now by Brembo and provide stunning stopping power.

There were two levels of interior trim – 'Luxury', with piped leather seats, and 'Sports', that featured cloth inserts to the sports seats.

The rear spoiler and massive rear tyres look very purposeful.

The luxury model's leather cabin.

The Sport 300 in action! Courtesy of Lotus Cars.

1996–98: The Sport 300

This was a derivative of the X180R racer. It weighs in at 250 lbs less than the S4s and still packs 300 bhp from the chargecooled engine; the head being reworked and ported and the chargecooler capacity enlarged. The seats are Recaro race seats, the interior trim alcantara and cloth, and the bodywork mods from the X180R include the front spoiler and wheelarch extensions. The brakes are AP racing callipers and the tyres Goodyear GS-Cs on 10.5 inch x 17 inch rear and 8.5 inch x 16 inch front OZ racing alloys. Its track credentials were proven with the provision of a track package, including a roll cage.

1996: The Esprit GT1

This was Type 114 in Lotus model codes. It was the next step from the X180R, using the V8 engine to step up to GT1 racing. Lack of development time and funds meant reliability issues plagued the car.

The V8 racer that proved too unreliable – looks great though! Picture courtesy of Lotus Cars.

1996–98: The V8 Esprit

The first production Lotus V8 road car arrived in 1996. The Esprit V8 is powered by the Lotus-designed 3.5 litre twin turbocharged V8 engine.

This engine started on the drawing board for the Corvette. It was the product of cutting edge design. As Lotus explained in their brochure, the engine was 'efficient, compact and lightweight — weighing less than 220 kg complete with all ancillaries.' It produced up to 350 bhp (260 kW) at 6,500 rpm and gave the Esprit V8 acceleration times of: 0–100 km/h (0–62 mph) in 4.9 seconds, 0–160 km/h in 10.3 seconds (0–100 mph in 10.54 seconds), before reaching a certified top speed of 280km/h (175 mph). It also boasted a wide torque band with a peak of 400 Nm (295 lb/foot) at 4,250 rpm. Smooth power delivery produced an effortless and rapid acceleration in all five gears. I can attest to this extremely rapid progress when during my first drive of a V8 I had to jink violently right to miss the rear of the van I was overtaking, when the power of the V8 blasted me forwards like it had rocket boosters!

Specifications: (1996)

Engine: 3,506 cc all aluminium, 90-degree V8, longitudinal, mid-mounted, with twin Allied Signal T25 turbochargers

Max Power: 355 bhp (260kW) at 6500 rpm Maximum torque: 295 lb/foot (400 Nm) at 4250 rpm

Gearbox: 5-speed manual

Chassis: Steel backbone with rear tubular structure

A U.S. specification V8 in white with chromed alloys.

A V8 engine and gearbox.

Front Suspension: Double-wishbones, single coil springs, telescopic dampers, anti-roll bar
Rear Suspension: Upper and lower transverse links, box section radius arms, telescopic dampers with coil springs
Wheels: OZ Racing six-spoke monobloc alloy Front: 8.5Jx17 Rear: 10.0Jx18
Tyres: Dunlop SP Sport 9000 Front: 235/40 ZR17 Rear: 285/35 ZR18
Brakes: Front – Brembo 4 Pot front callipers, 11.6 inch (296 mm) diameter discs
Rear – Brembo 2 pot callipers, 12.0 inch (300mm) diameter discs
Weight: 3,040 lb (1,380 kg)
0–60 mph: 4.9 secs
Max Speed: 175 mph
Wheelbase: 95.3 inches (2,420 mm)
Front track: 59.8 inches (1,520 mm)
Rear track: 59.8 inches (1,520 mm)
Overall length: 170.2 inches (4,369 mm)
Overall width: 74.1 inches (1,883 mm) excluding mirrors
Overall height: 45.3 inches (1,150 mm)
Ground clearance: 4.1 inches (105 mm)

The V8-GT weighs in some 40 kg less than the V8 and without some of the styling and interior detailing; there is no rear wing, for instance. The price was less than the other models and as such a little more tempting to prospective owners.

The Esprit V8 engine bay, showing how small the engine actually is.

1998–2001: The V8-SE

This model has the same mechanicals and specifications as the other V8 models but has a higher interior and luxury specification.

The V8's impressively upgraded interior. Picture courtesy of Lotus Cars.

A 2002 model V8 at Hethel. Courtesy of Lotus Cars.

1999: The Sport 350

Visually altered from the Esprit V8-SE and GT to include a newly-styled front end and a huge carbon fibre rear wing on aluminium uprights, designed around a similar wing worn by the Type 115 GT racer. 350 decals appear on the doors and roof.

Above: The Sport 350 at Donnington.

Right: Car number 000, with the last styling change to the rear of the V8s.

Note the light alloy wheels and rear spoiler.

Sporting and stylish interior.

New OZ Racing alloy wheels with Pirelli tyres increase grip and reduce weight whilst beneath the exterior, larger AP Racing brakes improve stopping power. Stiffer suspension and engine bracing provides extra rigidity. Revised mapping of the ECU system produces an increase in torque in the three lower gears, and a reduce kerb weight of 80 kg makes this the most accelerative Esprit in history. A limited number of fifty were to be built and all true 350s will have a blue engine cover rather than the normal V8 red cover.

Specifications:
Max power: 349 bhp at 6,500 rpm
Max torque: 295 lb/foot at 4,250 rpm
Brakes: Front 12.6 inch (320 mm) drilled and ventilated discs Rear 12.6 inch (320 mm) drilled and ventilated discs
0–60 mph: 4.7 seconds
Max Speed: 175 mph
Unladen Weight: 2,866 lbs (1,300 kg)

2002–03: The S2 V8

The S2 was introduced with revised styling to the rear in particular (by Russell Carr), with round rear lights and more lavish interior fittings. The aluminium look of the Elise being brought about in the Esprit's luxury cabin. At £49,995, it was a bargain supercar. The Kelsey-Hayes ABS was an upgrade and the alloys were specially designed to aid cooling of the AP racing discs.

One of the last specification V8s.

The changes to the rear lights and moving the exhaust pipes to the centre.

The final US spec. cars have the twin exhaust pipes centrally mounted as in the Elise. Production ceased in 2003.

3

Buyer's Guide

If you know you want to but you just don't know what you are getting into, here is some advice on what to buy and what to expect – and inspect – before you do. First of all, are you looking for something rare and sought-after, or do you have a yearning for a certain model? Initially have a look at our Model History and decide where your heart is taking you, then read on and let your wallet have a say!

This guide is just that; it is a culmination of many years of experience in buying and owning Lotus cars but, ultimately, it is only a guide – your decision to buy is yours alone. The guide breaks the Esprit down into the various series and the significant re-engineering points of the model over the years, outlining the improvements. Of course, buyers of the Esprit marque generally have a favourite model before they even start looking for a car to buy, so hopefully this guide will show you generally what to look for on the model of your choice. However, if you are a general enthusiast of the marque and have a limited budget or want to choose the model based upon reliability improvements, then this guide should also help you make a more informed choice. We have tried to list some of the most common issues to look out for. Though some issues run throughout the Esprit production to the very end, such as rusting petrol tanks, some issues are model-specific.

The sought-after models tend to be the following ones. They are not listed in any particular order, other than possibly chronologically:

Guigiaro Esprits: All of the S1 cars, the S2 JPS Ltd Edition, the S2.2, the Essex Commemorative Turbo Esprit, Early Turbo Esprit dry sump models fitted with Compomotive alloy wheels, Turbo Esprit HC and Turbo Esprit HC commemorative edition.

Stevens Esprits: The 40th Commemorative, the Sport 300, the S4s, the V8 GT350 and very last production cars.

It is true that all of the Guigiaro cars have rocketed in value in recent years, as have the other rarities, however it is worth noting that although some models are sought-after, that does not necessarily mean that they are the best Esprits in terms of driving experience, value for money, nor reliability.

You need to know that, like all Lotus cars from the early Elite, through to the Elise in 1996, the Esprit's basic construction is in two parts; the steel backbone chassis, which is the platform for suspension, engine, and transmission, and the body, which is fibreglass and sits upon the chassis to house the occupants and look wonderful.

Series 1, 2 and S2.2

We have placed these models together because they are basically very similar in construction, using the same chassis design.

The S1 cars are very sought after these days primarily because of the Bond film *The Spy Who Loved Me*, where the Esprit showcased to the world its stunning futuristic looks, superb handling, and aquatic abilities as a submarine. Although typical of all Lotus road cars, the early models tend not to have all the day to day running issues – these are sorted before being released for sale to the general public.

General points to look out for relating to the S1, S2, and S2.2:

Body

The bodies of all models of Esprit are generally excellent in strength and surface finish. The body does not tend to suffer from stress cracks as a result of day to day fatigue, unlike the earlier '60s Lotus model range, where the fibreglass is much thinner. The improvements in quality and strength of this generation of Lotus road cars can be in the main attributed to the Lotus developed VARI system of fibreglass body manufacture; a system whose basic principles are still used by Lotus today.

When looking at any Esprit you still need to check for stress cracks or 'crazing' on the fibreglass bodywork, as this could be signs of previous accident damage. Light cracks near the bumpers, door edges, and headlamp pod apertures are not uncommon. These cracks

Crazing around a frontal area 'knock'.

Crazing around the light pods is quite common.

A replacement Esprit chassis.

are usually related to parking nudges and doors being bumped against objects when being opened, rather than any serious accident damage.

A classic sign of badly repaired accident damage can be seen by looking at the black plastic waist trim that runs down either side of the centre of the car doors wings and rear quarters. The trim should be un-rippled, level, even, and follow a smooth curve around the wheel arches. Poor repairs are often highlighted by poorly fitting waist trim.

Chassis

The S1, S2 and S2.2 have the same chassis; the only difference being the S2.2's chassis is galvanised so it does not suffer the same problems as the S1 and S2 chassis, detailed below.

The S1and S2 chassis are mild steel and were only coated in a thin coat of black paint, with the inevitable consequence that they are susceptible to rust in various places. The front chassis suspension pick-up points and spring turrets in particular need to be checked for excessive rust. The front high 'T' section – high up where the body sits on a foam saddle on top of the chassis – also needs to be checked.

The rear chassis space frame tubes, in particular the top rail on the near side, which runs very close to the exhaust manifold, needs particular attention as this is susceptible to corrosion and severe pitting at the closest point to the exhaust manifold and around the tube leading to the vertical chassis box that mounts the trialling arm bush.

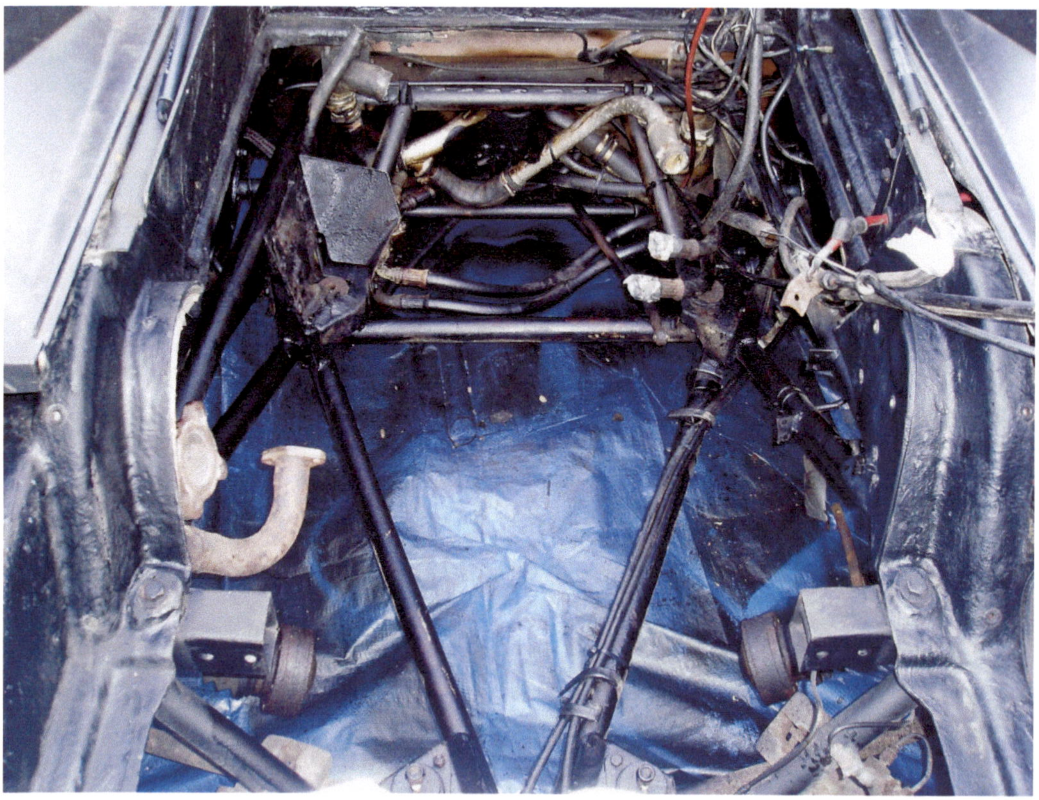

The chassis tubes with the engine removed.

The exhaust pipe curling around the susceptible chassis tubes.

Check the tube from the wheelarch side where it runs closest to the exhaust manifold.

The rear spring turret on a galvanised car; check all around the area and brush off all loose material.

Esprit rear suspension showing the spring turret and the chassis bars above the brake disc.

Front suspension in good condition.

Again rear suspension turrets need to be checked. The same checks should be carried out on the S2.2 to make sure the galvanised coating has not been compromised. If the galvanised coating has been damaged, check to make sure this is not the result of physical accident damage and that corrosion has not set in.

If the chassis is excessively rusty, this is a major issue that cannot be easily rectified and could potentially require a new chassis with all of the associated time and labour costs!

Engine

The S1 and S2 use the Lotus 907 2-litre engine, while the S2.2 uses the larger-capacity 912 2.2-litre replacement for the 907. However, the checks listed below apply to both types of engine.

The 907 engine provides adequate performance in healthy condition and if serviced correctly is generally reliable, while the 912 provides more performance through increased torque and also, surprisingly, improved fuel economy.

Cambelts need monitoring and changing at least at the specified mileage or when they are five years old. Most of the 907 engine failures in service in later years can be attributed to cambelt failures due to incorrect servicing or the complete lack of it. In particular, the engines fitted with a spring-loaded semi-automatic tensioner can suffer

An Esprit S2 907 engine with the older cam covers.

from worn bushes on the tensioner pivot, which can alter the position of the belt on the cam, crank and auxiliary sprockets, damaging or causing adverse wear to the cambelt. This can lead to belt failure and result in serious internal engine damage. Incorrect belt tension can also cause adverse wear if too tight, or jumping of the belt if not tight enough, throwing the engine out of mechanical timing – again resulting in serious internal engine damage. If a car has not had a recent cam belt change then factor this cost into buying the car.

I would avoid driving a car any distance without proof of a cambelt service within the recommended time and mileage service interval. The same checks apply to the Esprit engine as would apply to any other car; watch for excessive blue smoke indicating a worn, oil burning engine. Check the oil dip stick for a caramel-type coating indicating oil and water mixing, suggesting a head gasket or piston liner seal failure. When starting any 900 series Lotus engine, an amount of mechanical engine noise caused by piston slap is quite normal. This should quieten significantly as the engine warms.

Run the engine up to operating temp on a test drive and check the engine does not overheat. This again could indicate a head gasket failure coupled with other tell-tale signs detailed above. The Lotus 900 series engines do tend to use oil so do not be too concerned if a car uses typically 1 litre of oil per 500 miles.

The 907 engine with the carburettors removed to show the distributor, oil filter and alternator.

An Achilles heel of the 900 series carburettor-equipped engine design is the position of the carburettors directly over the distributor and close to the alternator. This makes servicing awkward but, more importantly, it makes any fuel leak from the carbs a serious fire hazard.

Carburettors – and fuel supply pipes to them – need to be inspected for damage and any signs of leaks (such as damp patches or fuel smells). Carburettor overhauls are, however, not overly expensive and can be done by skilled amateurs. There are excellent books detailing what is required in an overhaul.

The camshaft covers are of a saddle type (as they sit on top of the cam holders) and can be prone to oil leaks. This can fill the spark plug area with oil. This issue is addressed on later models with the introduction of improved cam carriers with flat panel cam covers; again not a serious problem but something to be aware of, even if you do not need to be overly concerned about it.

A fuel smell in the cabin when driving can be caused by fuel leakage in the engine bay as detailed earlier. However, a common cause can be a fuel tank breather pipe, which runs across the cabin rear bulkhead between the two fuel tanks. Also, the rubber seals on the fuel caps can become shrunken and no longer seal, allowing fuel vapour smells in the cabin – especially if a window is open or after refilling.

A more serious issue causing fuel smell can be caused by leaking fuel tanks. The tanks sit on foam and were only covered in a thin coat of black paint, so are susceptible to rust. Inspection of the tanks can be achieved by removing the rear quarter window shelves in the engine compartment and plywood covers. Access to the underside of the tanks can also be gained by raising the car up and removing the rubber inspection plugs on the quarter sills. Replacement of the tanks is not an easy job and tanks are not cheap. If for any reason the engine has to be removed it is prudent to check the fuel tanks at this time, as access is improved greatly with the engine removed.

Gearbox

The Esprit used a Citroen SM Transaxle all through the Giugiaro-designed cars' production. These gearboxes have a few faults to be aware of. Externally, an oil leak from the rear-most gearbox cover where the Esprit rear silencer is mounted is not uncommon and is easily resealed with new sealant. However, your concern should be whether the car has been driven for many miles low on gearbox lubricant because of this type of common leak. Second gear synchromesh can be weak, signalled by crunching into second gear when down-shifting. The crown wheel and pinion can become damaged, however, and this is more of an issue with the more powerful Turbo Esprit. Repairs of this type of gearbox are costly and parts can be in short supply.

This is an unusual state for one of Mike's Esprits, but it shows the engine installed in the S2 chassis and the gearbox to the rear.

If the car you are looking at shows any signs of gearbox problems, factor this into the price of the car. If the gear change seems vague or sloppy, this is normally due to worn bushes in the linkage, which are very inexpensive and easy to change or, better still, upgrade.

Clutch 'Red Tube' Issues

A problem for all Esprit models through the years has been the red, flexible plastic tube that supplies hydraulic fluid from the clutch reservoir at the front of the Esprit to the rear slave cylinder in the engine bay. The engine bay of an Esprit can get to be quite a hot place, especially on the turbo models, causing the red flexible pipe to expand when under hydraulic pressure and thus not forcing the full amount of fluid through to the slave cylinder and, in doing so, not fully disengaging the clutch. This causes difficulty in engaging gears, especially when in traffic when the engine bay is at its hottest. A braided clutch line is the solution to this problem. These are readily available through Lotus specialists, are easily fitted, and are inexpensive.

Interior

Lotus interiors are not the hardest-wearing of automobiles; however, the most common issues in this era of Esprit tend to be caused by age and/or long-term storage whilst unused. Head-linings and sun visors tend to deteriorate and sag but these are easily DIY-restored or repaired, or can be re-trimmed by a coach trimmer at a reasonable price. The head-lining covering materials

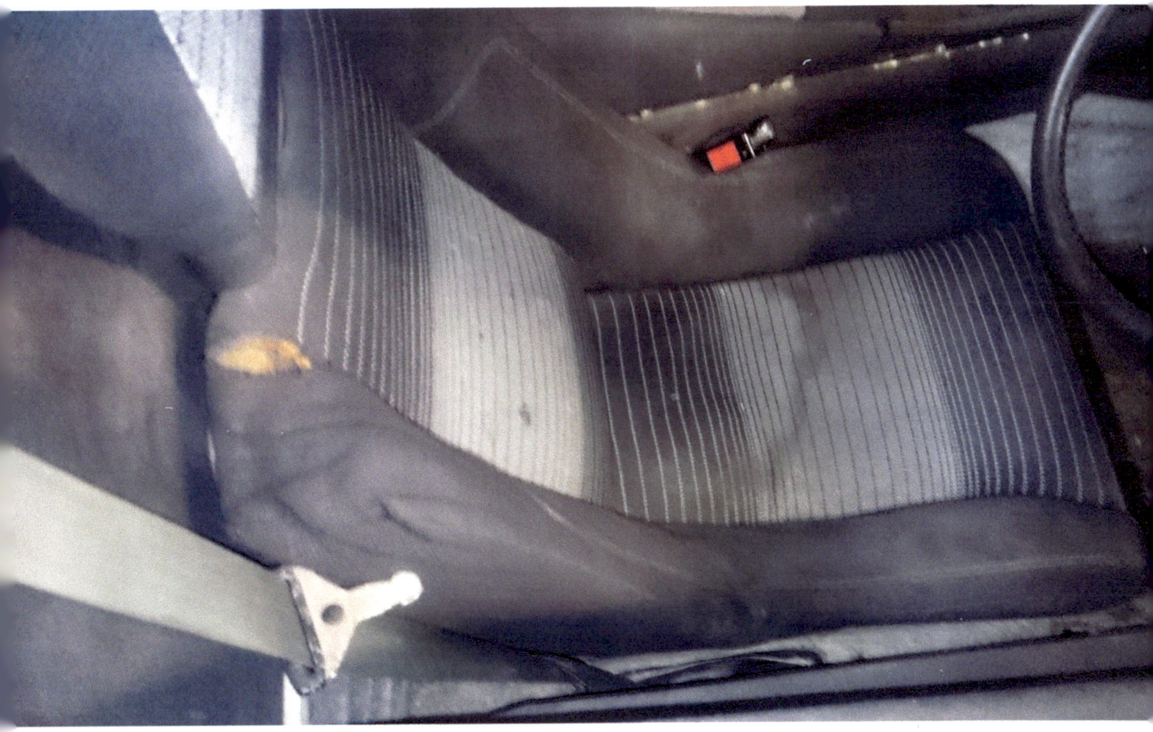

Seats that have seen better days and will need more than just cleaning; re-trimming is in order.

are readily available through such companies as Woollies. Seats, carpets and door cards can be recovered at reasonable cost, though recovering the Esprit dash can be costly; mainly because of the labour time involved in removing and refitting. If you want your car to be as perfect as the day it left the factory, N. Fulcher Trimmers have to be considered the trimmers to use.

The Lotus factory experience and factory patterns handed down through the company have produced some jaw-dropping results from this company. We cannot comment on the costs involved in this type of restoration as your choice of company and level of re-trim will be factored in to costs.

Door cards can come apart if completely neglected.

Carpets in the Esprit are not difficult to fit and are quite reasonably priced, but the handbrake gaiter...

Dashboards are not easy to re-trim so leave it to the experts.

It must be pointed out the interiors of cars that have been well looked-after all their lives tend to fare very well, and a good interior can be a good indication of a pampered Esprit. Always try careful and painstaking cleaning before you think about re-trimming.

Suspension and Steering

The suspension on the Esprit S1 through to S2.2 was unchanged and can be considered quite robust for a car of this type. Any sign of vagueness in steering or nervous handling are signs of worn bushes or steering components. These are not seriously expensive issues. All Esprits should handle superbly and be very communicative on the move. Often over-heavy steering can simply be caused by the universal joint connecting the steering column to the steering rack, which can partially seize on cars that have been stored for a while. Rear wheel bearings are also a common weak spot as they are Austin Maxi front wheel bearings and are at the limit of their engineering design in this application. This is due to the poor design of the rear suspension placing stress on a number of components and therefore leading to adverse wear if not serviced correctly. The drive shaft universal joints in particular if not regularly greased can wear quickly, placing stress on the wheel bearings. Springs and dampers are available from aftermarket companies, but careful setup of these units is required as they tend to be adjustable. Attaining the original dynamics of the Esprit while retaining the excellent ride characteristics is almost impossible with aftermarket parts; however the original parts are now no longer available so this is the only option. This is an area where the forums can be very helpful as other owners will no doubt have done some of the development work for you!

Brakes

The brakes on the Esprit are not comprised of specialist parts so can be maintained and restored at a very reasonable cost. Only the rear discs and rear brake callipers cost a little more than a standard classic car. The brakes should stop the car well with no fade judder or pulling to either side. Brake pipes should be inspected carefully on cars without a current MOT certificate.

Electrics

When new, the early series of Esprit were not particularly known for the reliability of their electrics and if you now factor in the age of the car, this is something you may have to learn to live with. Always check the wiring thoroughly before spending money buying new or reconditioned parts, as many of the electrical faults can be traced to poor earth connections as the type of build, using various chassis earth points, is not ideal. This is obviously because, unlike most modern cars, the fibreglass body is non-conductive. Headlamp lift and operation problems are again often earth related, or can be traced to the various relays used to operate the headlamp lifting motors and switch the lamps on. Most electrical components were sourced from other manufacturers' parts bins by Lotus and this continued throughout the Esprit's production. There are many good online lists of parts cross-references and specialist suppliers.

Series 3 and Turbo Esprit S3

Body

Please see the guide for the S1, S2 and S2.2 as the S3 body is for the most part the same as the earlier models.

The Turbo version can suffer damage to the front lower spoiler from high kerb stones and the like, and the rear flip-up spoiler does tend to suffer paint damage on its upper, most prominent lip. This often happens during accessing the engine bay for servicing, when you must lean over the spoiler lip to reach into the engine bay. Later versions of the S3 have the option of a lift-out glass roof, which can be stored in a bag in the boot. This gives the cabin an airier feel and gives extra head room for taller drivers.

Chassis

The Series 3 chassis is a vast improvement on the S1 to S2.2, allowing all-new rear suspension. It is galvanised, so rust is not such a concern, however still check the chassis for areas where the galvanised coating has been compromised and inspect closely for physical accident damage.

Engine

The majority of normally aspirated Esprit S3s used the 2.2-litre, 912 engine as per the S2.2 – details of which can be found in the previous S2.2 guide. This engine from approximately 1983 onwards benefitted from revised cam carriers, which much improved the oil leakage issues. The very last non-turbo S3 used a high compression version of the 2.2, 912 engine, which is proven to be a more durable, reliable, and smooth engine if serviced correctly. The

HC engine, as it was called, uses a HTD profile on the cambelt sprockets, allowing the car to have longer service intervals between belt changes.

910 Turbo Engine

The Turbo 900 series engine is quite different to the normally aspirated engine with its own particular issues.

Early dry sump cars are very sought-after at present, however parts for the oil pump are scarce and this engine did cause a number of problems when in production; much of which centred around new owners not understanding how to check and therefore maintain the correct oil levels. The dry sump was quickly phased out after a little over a year of production and less than 200 cars.

All the 910 engines in low compression form use Hepolite pistons, which are easily damaged if production specification boost is exceeded for any reason. The engine gained a fragile reputation because of the external waste gate sticking closed, thus greatly exceeding the safe boost level and melting the piston crown. Unfortunately, the position of the waste gate does leave it exposed to the elements and it can easily seize closed – especially if the

Turbo engine and gearbox with turbo and manifold visible. Note the protection for the spoiler lip.

car has been laid up for a little while. When test driving a Turbo Esprit *gently* accelerate and watch the boost gauge rise; don't allow it to increase quickly past the safe boost limit. With the window slightly down watch the boost gauge rise gently then back *completely off* the throttle. Listen for the turbo whistle while spinning up as the boost rises, then there should be a sudden gasp, thump, and then flutter of the waste gate as it dumps excess boost when the throttle is lifted off. If there is not this sound and the boost only gradually subsides, this is a sure sign of a sticking waste gate. By testing the car in this way, at least you should not have damaged the engine. Drive the car no further until the waste gate receives attention. This can be a simple procedure if the waste gate can be unbolted and freed off relatively easily but if the bolts on the waste gate are seized this can involve a lot of other remedial work in the process, so bargain hard if the car has this fault as this could be quite a costly repair (unless the exhaust manifold and waste gate adapter have already been recently replaced). Exhaust manifolds do have a tendency to crack so check any exhaust blowing noise is not in fact a manifold issue. Make sure the Turbo oil feed supply pipes are in good, leak-free condition. Excessive blue smoke under boost can signal a worn turbo charger. The usual engine tests as detailed in the earlier S1 to S2.2 guide should also be checked.

The cambelt and pulleys on the Turbo 910 engine. There is very little clearance when still in the car.

The later HC turbo engine is a much more robust specification engine, utilising Mahle pistons and Nikasil liners and a revised turbocharger. The pistons can take a lot more punishment than the early pistons so engines tend to be more reliable and longer-lasting. Again, the HTD cam pulleys fitted to the HC engine allow longer service intervals.

Gearbox

The Citroen SM gearbox is unchanged from the earlier cars except for a different bell housing to incorporate a slightly larger clutch and slave cylinder. The extra torque and power of the turbo engine can cause problems with the crown wheel and pinion and also second gear synchromesh. Parts are at a premium for this type of gearbox.

Interior

The interior is the same as in the S1 to S2.2 cars.

Suspension and Steering

Again, please reference the guide for the S1 to S2.2 cars.

The rear suspension on the series 3 car is quite different to the S1 through to S2.2 cars and is much more desirable with all the previous problems resolved.

Brakes

Again the brakes on the Esprit Series 3 are not constituted of specialist parts and so can be maintained and restored at a very reasonable cost, with only the rear discs and rear brake callipers costing a little more than a standard classic car. The brakes should stop the car well with no fade judder or pulling to either side.

Electrics

These are as for the S1 to S2.2 models.

The Stevens-Styled Esprit

X180 Normally Aspirated & Esprit Turbo (Carburettor Model)

The Stevens Esprit is essentially a re-body of the last spec HC S3 Giugairio models. There are a few differences to be aware of, making the car again a step forward in addressing weaknesses of the last Guigario-styled cars.

Body

The body was completely new, however dimensionally it kept to within 1 inch of the original cars' dimensions. The same damage checks apply as with previous models.

Chassis

The chassis is the same as the previous S3 with slight dimensional changes and therefore should be checked in the same manner as the earlier S3 cars.

Engine

The engine is largely unchanged from the previous S3 HC cars. However, the turbo model benefits from a new water-cooled turbo with integral waste gate, which is a huge step forward from the previous, badly positioned waste gate, and resolves many of the sticking waste gate issues. However, this should still be checked as detailed in the S3 guide, as all Esprits tend to be stored for long periods of time between use, which can cause moving parts to stick on any make or model of car.

Gearbox

A completely different Renault transaxle is used for the Stevens Esprit. This unit is more robust than the Citroen SM unit, however it is not without fault and should be checked in the same way as the Citroen SM unit. A stiff or vague gear change can be caused by the selector on the rear of the gearbox and is a common issue as the rubber covers fail; allowing the elements in and seizing the selector bearings. An upgrade is available that greatly improves the gear change. A tricky repair more than an expensive problem.

Interior

The Stevens-styled cars have a slightly increased interior size and benefit from rake adjustable seats and lift-out roof as standard fitment, but the advice on the interior is the same as previous models.

Suspension and Steering

This area is the same as for the S3 models.

Brakes

These are the same as for previous models.

Esprit SE (Fuel Injected)

All the general guides for the Stevens X180 and Esprit Turbo apply to the SE.

The SE signalled a leap forward in performance with the fuel injected engine. In standard specification the SE came fitted with a costly catalytic converter that, as far as UK regulations are concerned, was not necessary, so many owners fit a de-cat pipe and also remove the EBP valve from the exhaust system as it was prone to sticking, improving performance.

As part of the package to increase power, Lotus fitted a 'Chargecooler' (basically a water cooled intercooler). This has a rather fragile mechanical pump fitted where earlier models used to have their distributor. To test if this pump is functioning, after a test drive place the palm of your hand on top of the chargecooler, which sits on top of the engine proclaiming itself with 'chargecooler' written on the top. If the chargecooler feels hot, the pump has failed. A lot of people replace the mechanical pump with an electric water circulation pump.

Engine misfires are often caused by failing ignition coil packs. These are commonly sourced items from the General Motors parts bin, which were also used on Isuzu Troopers and Vauxhall Carlton and Senator models. Being fuel injected also means the SE is the first Esprit to have an electronic means for diagnosis of engine management issues. The front of the SE is laden with radiators for engine cooling, chargecooler, air conditioning, and oil coolers. This, coupled with larger wheels, wider-profile tyres and no power steering, can make the steering on the heavy side when parking. The steering racks are also put under more strain and so can be prone to wear. The last of the SE model were fitted with what was known as the 'High Wing', but there were not many 'High Wing' variants made. Some new buyers of the SE specified their new Esprit not to be fitted with the wing in the first place, while later owners had them simply removed, making 'High Wings' somewhat of a rarity these days.

Esprit S4, S4s, GT3

The Esprit development marched on with the Esprit model range dropping carburettors completely for fuel injection and introducing power steering, ABS, and a more rounded profile of bumpers, side sill profiles, and different rear spoilers.

New issues now come to light. In general, the S4 model range is mostly the same as the SE in terms of what to look out for. However, as the Esprit ages and has been out of production for some time, certain essential components have become obsolete for the more complicated Esprit models.

The Delco ABS system fitted to the S4 through to the first V8 Esprit can cause serious problems as it ages and parts are no longer available. A key issue is the pressure switch. When this fails it throws on the ABS warning light, making your car unable to pass an MOT. This switch has been obsolete for a number of years. Some owners have managed to simply remove the switch and flush and clean the switch internals to get it working again.

The brake servo system in the S4s is to the right of the tiny spare.

A Lotus specialist in Australia has developed a system using two new switches, but this will cost you well over £500 to buy and ship to the UK. I had this problem on an S4s. Unfortunately the switch was broken and irreparable so another Esprit owner and I set about returning the car back to standard brakes without ABS. This is completely legal and actually improved the brakes. I will supply more information about this on our website.

Esprit V8

The Esprit V8 takes the model into the serious super-car league and as such the maintenance costs can also be in another league. Having said this, if you buy a good example and maintain it correctly there should be few problems. There are many very happy V8 owners out there who will tell you that what costs there are are worth it for the driving experience.

The Esprit V8 essentially took up where the S4s ended in terms of looks, interior trim, brakes and the like. However, the V8 engine installation has its own problems and if you are set on buying a V8 I suggest you do your homework on the model and the vehicle you are planning to purchase thoroughly as engine, clutch, and gearbox repairs are extremely costly. In particular, the earlier V8 cars have a reputation for engine failures due to liner sealing problems. However, Lotus went to great lengths to investigate and rectify this issue. Lotus found the liner sealing issue was caused by the engines in question having been overheated at some point, thus causing the liner sealer to fail. From 2000 onwards a different, improved sealer was used, but Lotus still maintain the original liner sealer is fine, provided the engine is never overheated.

Weak header tank caps, coolant leakages, blocked radiators and water pump pulley issues have been known to cause overheating issues, which subsequently lead to the V8 liner sealant issues.

A V8 Anniversary edition Esprit.

The V8 engine out of the car. So compact!

An Esprit 350 engine – note the blue cam covers. The price on the ticket says £3,995 and that was in the mid-noughties!

The V8 torque also puts a lot of stress on the Renault-sourced transaxle and clutch. Later V8 models use a multi plate clutch, which improved the life of the clutch and gave it a lighter pedal feel. Some earlier cars had the twin plate clutch retro fitted. However, this also significantly increases clutch replacement costs.

Lotus catalytic converters fitted to V8s only last about three years; first they start to rattle and then they fall apart. They are £900 + VAT and fitting, each! Non-Lotus catalysts are available and are significantly cheaper. Heatshields can rattle, sounding like a multitude of problems, but this is not a serious issue.

During 1998 the Esprit cabin was revised with a simpler dash arrangement, which also yielded more knee room for taller drivers. This tends to make the later dash models more sought after. After 2000, AP brakes were fitted to Esprits that further increased brake maintenance costs. As with previous models, check the braking power and for pulling to either side – the stopping power should be prodigious!

The Buying Experience

So you may have made up your mind about the model you want by now. Here are some generic tips and things to look out for, whatever model you are thinking about, when you go to look at a prospective bargain.

A great number of Lotus cars that come up for sale have been stored or laid-up for quite a long time. The first thing to consider is why the car was stored or left unused in the first place. Reasons vary from mechanical failure – sometimes this seemed worse than it in fact turned out and the car was taken off the road for little reason, but sometimes the cause was serious and leaving the car to stand without preparing it properly has added to the problems – to, rarely, but it does happen, the owner simply had a personal problem that has left the car inactive; Esprits can be very difficult to get in and out of if you have a sudden back problem, for instance! Occasionally the owner dies and the family find it hard to part with the beloved Lotus!

There are areas to look at before you try to start a car that has been standing for a long time, let alone try to drive it.

The Engine

If you know the engine has not been started in a considerable time do not rush the process! Make sure you have a healthy battery. If you don't have a meter to check it, recharge it as a matter of course.

Drain the engine oil – it has probably become contaminated and it isn't worth the risk that it was 'old' before the engine was laid-up. Remove the oil filter as well and drain the oil cooler if you can. Make sure the entire engine drains overnight and then fit a new filter. We would recommend taking out the plugs and checking gaps and condition. If there is any doubt about their condition, get new ones. A little light oil (three in one, WD40 etc.) dripped or sprayed into the cylinders through the spark plug holes may help if the engine has stood for considerable time, or has been neglected and out of the car. Don't flood the cylinders with oil! Leave the plugs out and try turning the engine slowly at the crank pulley.

If the engine sticks at any point when you are turning it over, stop immediately and start looking to strip the engine down, even partially, to discover what is coming into contact with what! You will probably save yourself the price of a new engine.

If the engine turns through 720 degrees, two revolutions, and appears to be free of mechanical restrictions, you can try the next part. Leaving the plugs out, replace the battery and check the coolant levels and belts for the alternator and water-pump. Push the belts inward at their longest point and they should deflect slightly (about 0.5 inches).

Make sure you inspect the cam-belt closely. It should be flexible and be free from cracks and damage. It is always better to put a new cam-belt on before you try to run an engine that has been standing unused for a long length of time. The belt can become brittle, and spending a long time in one position can give it a problem with its shape (just like the tyres). The last thing you want is to start the engine for the first time and hear the belt snap and valves smashing into pistons!

We also recommend you remove the main coil to distributor lead and tie back the spark plug leads safely. You can now turn the engine over on the starter to check that it is reasonably mechanically sound and that all the major parts are at least doing their jobs in some coherent fashion.

If all is still well, you can move on to actually trying to start the engine. First, replace the spark plugs and lead to the distributor and put several gallons of petrol in the tank. If there is a substantial amount of petrol already in the tank, try to ensure that a good proportion of the petrol available to the engine is new, as petrol can go 'off'. The aromatics in modern petrol evaporate away, reducing the octane rating considerably, and this will affect your engine's ability to run at all, never mind smoothly. If you sit in the driving seat and turn the ignition to the point before engaging the starter motor you should be able to actually hear the petrol pump running and building fuel pressure to the carburettors.

This is a two-man job from here on in! Remove the car from the garage and make sure you have a fire extinguisher or the like handy. Leave the bonnet open. Go through the normal start-up procedure and attempt to start the engine. There is usually a bit of coughing and stuttering and it may take a while for the petrol to pump through from the tank, although if you are attempting the restart after the previous operations, this should already have happened.

If the engine starts, one of you should check all around the engine for any kind of leaks or problems that can be detected in the engine bay. Running the engine at about 1,500 to 2,000 rpm should be sufficient to do this check. It is a good idea to monitor the coolant level during this period of warm up; the level may drop as the thermostat opens and allows the coolant to circulate, so top it up if necessary.

Keep an eye on the temperature gauge once the engine is started; as it begins to rise you may try a few more revs. If there are any suspicious noises turn the engine off as soon as possible and investigate.

The 907, 912 and 910 Lotus engines can be a little 'clattery' on start up as they warm through. This is nothing to be concerned about. However, if the noises continue after the temperature gauge nears normal operating temperature, you may require some further engine work. Noisy tappets will require renovation and adjustment.

Don't leap in too early and try to move the car on the engine as you will need to have checked the operation of brakes, steering, clutch and gears before you go for actual movement. It is no use being able to go if you can't stop or steer!

You can then go on to check the compression using a suitable gauge. Next check the engine timing through the hatch on the clutch bellhousing, using a xenon timing light. It is a good idea to put some 'Redex' petrol treatment, or 'Forte' general additive through the petrol system by adding them to the tank. The latter treatment does an amazing job of cleaning carburettor internals and can really make the engine run better without further dismantling and cleaning. Remember you won't necessarilly find out if there are problems with oil lines, petrol lines, water hoses or the electrical system until you actually move the car and put it through a road test, but that's another story.

Safety first – look at the tyres. Remember you are looking at a high performance sports car that was specifically designed to work best on a particular make and size of tyre; Lotus are that specific in their development. So, while it may sound wonderful when the present owner tells you that the car has the original tyres still on the car, it is anything but. It would probably be lethal! Even a well-known television car-dealing duo sold an Esprit that had Goodyear tyres that were deleted from production before 2000 – no wonder the car was sideways throughout the drive around Lotus' test track!

The last Esprits were built in 2003, so the tyres will be fourteen years old by now and well past their sell-by date. Modern tyres have a shelf life of about six to eight, or possibly

Make sure you check the tyres thoroughly; this crack could be facing downwards!

ten years if they are used regularly and looked after, because even if they have done very few miles, the rubber degrades and they become harder (like old cheddar) and are subsequently less flexible. This means that at every revolution of the tyre, the deformation and expansion as the tread meets the road leads to cracks and fractures – possibly hidden inside the tyre. This will lead to weakness where the tread is welded to the carcass of the tyre and the first you may know about this degradation is when you take your new toy for a spirited excursion and the tread parts company with the tyre with disastrous effect. It could be the finish of both of you.

There is a DOT code on the side of the tyre. If the code is only three digits long, the tyre is far too old (originating before 2000). If it has four digits, you can read the date the tyre was manufactured in the following manner: the first two digits refer to the week number of the year it was made and the second two digits refer to the year so, for example, 3610 would mean the 36th week of 2010.

The age of the tyres should not unduly affect your decision to actually buy the car, but it should be a bargaining point and certainly a safety point.

There are two models of Esprit that came with split-rim alloy wheels as standard items. The early Esprit Turbo models (Essex models) had Compomotive split-rims and the later GT3, GT3s and S4s models also have bolted split-rim items fitted. You need to be aware that refurbishing this type of alloy is much more expensive than one-piece items and is generally only undertaken by specialists. At up to £500 per wheel, that could be a deal breaker when you are seeking to buy. Don't be tempted to unbolt and dismantle the wheels yourself to attempt a cheap fix! The wheel fixing bolts need to be meticulously re-torqued to ensure the stresses within the wheel are equal; if this is not done properly, the wheel could fail in use and cause a nasty accident.

4

Owning an Esprit

So you have taken the plunge and entered the world of ownership! There are some very simple and common-sense rules to owning any classic (or just old) car. I was watching a BBC 4 programme called *The Maharaja's Motor Car* recently and in the first six minutes of the programme a venerable Indian car collector, and descendant of a Maharaja, explained that 'cars need to be kept running'. No truer words have been spoken in advice to any classic car owner. He went on to say that his cars were, 'a thing of beauty,' and that he could, 'sit and watch all day and all night.' A wise man indeed, and what can be said about his Rolls-Royces can be perfectly applied to Lotuses.

Get a chair out and have a look at the car!

Cars are designed to run and move and be warmed through; to have all of their parts used and lubricated, and their batteries charged and the like. They are constructs of various types of metals and alloys and lubricants and fluids. If they are left to stand, some parts in particular will spend too long in contact with other parts and without movement or lubrication these will inevitably seize. Some fluids will begin to become an enemy to the parts they come into contact with (coolant, for example). A simple run out every two weeks or so will not only whet your appetite for life, but will also keep your pride and joy free of expensive problems with brakes, turbo wastegates, and the like. Then you can afford to sit and admire your beautiful investment 'all day and all night', as I know I have!

Above: A real beauty!

Right: This is the Scottish Motor Show car from 1985.

The commemorative plaque between the seats!

Caring for an Esprit

The Engine

If you know the engine is not going to be used for a considerable length of time, it is worth draining the coolant (the Esprit has some alloy pipework that would be better without constant contact with corrosive anti-freeze). Take the spark plugs out and spray the insides of the cylinders with WD40, and drip a little 3-in-one in as well. The engine being canted over, there will only be a proportion of the piston that will remain bathed in oil, but it is better than a completely dry cylinder. Put the plugs back in.

Battery

You will need a battery cut-off switch and a trickle charger. The expensive side of the trickle charger market is usually the likes of CTEK, which start at about £45. These are electronic-controlled devices that work very well and even have cold weather settings. However, in my considerable experience, the best value trickle chargers are made by Maypole and cost about £15. They do an excellent job for a third of the price of the high-end articles.

Just fit your cut-off switch to the end of the negative battery lead and you can leave the battery on the car. When you are not going to use the car for a while you simply unscrew the knob on the cut-out and it disconnects the battery. If you require security as well, you can unscrew the knob completely and take it with you, rendering the car immobile.

When you want to leave the battery on trickle charge, simply disconnect the battery from the car's electrical system with the cut-off and connect the trickle charger to the terminals on the battery. The trickle charger replicates the alternator in charging the battery, stopping the charge when it is fully charged and re-starting the charging when the battery charge drops away a little.

DO NOT try to charge a flat battery with a trickle charger, or you will need a new trickle charger – expensive or not! DO NOT connect a trickle charger to a battery that is still attached to the car's electricals or... you get the idea.

Brakes

When you store the car, do not leave the handbrake on. The pads will be in contact with the discs and they will probably seize to the discs eventually. Do not put the car away for any length of time after washing the car. It will be clean for when you come back to it, but it will just seize the brake pads to the discs and possibly help to corrode the pistons in the calipers if any of the seals are leaking. Store the car only when it is dry and having been driven. The heat will dry the brakes out and driving allows the pads to move away from the discs. Try not to use the brakes to stop the car in the garage; this will ensure a gap between the pads and the discs.

Ideally, and if a longer period of storage is required, jack the car up and free off the pads from the discs with a lever, carefully. If you can, make sure the handbrake linkages and cable are well-greased where they can be seen and where they require movement.

Tyres

Either jack the car up or keep it raised off the ground. The best way to do this is with axle stands on each corner, or other stabilising stands. You can alternatively use shaped rubber pads under the tyres to stop flat spots. There are specifically contoured pads called 'Tyre Trainers' that are available through retailers like Hamilton Classics. These follow the curve of the tyre and spread the weight of the car away from the contact patch to maintain the shape of the tyre.

Interior

Silicon bags (Thomar AirDry Car Dehumidifier Set) – these are bags full of silica cystals that attract and absorb water vapour, like the ones found in electrical packaging. Place them near the windscreens and centrally in the cabin. They will absorb moisture that condenses on the cold of the windscreens.

Use generous amounts of leather care cream – dry out the interior with the heater or a hot air blower before storing, and treat the leather.

Car Storage Covers and Cells

There are an extensive range of covers that are tailored to the Esprit shape. Everything from light interior covers that are primarilly to protect the bodywork from splashes and dust, to heavy, multilayered covers that are for outdoor use and protect against the effects of the sun on the paintwork and the environment upon the car as a whole. One of the primary threats to all classics when they are outside is bird strike! Bird poo eats paintwork and blisters the layers of paint if not removed as soon as humanly possible. I have experience of the lengths these avian critters will go to get at your Lotus – the crows this year decided that they would eat my expensive new cover and take strips away to line their nests!

There are prices to suit every pocket in the cover market, so shop carefully. Hamilton Classics have an extensive range and have been very reasonable when there have been problems with a cover.

What it should look like – from a Guigiaro, blue Esprit Turbo.

Car cells are expensive and, for me at least, not proven to help at all. Unless you use your garage for other things that are likely to constantly cover your beloved in harmful particles, a good lined interior cover will do the job as well. I am sure that my 'Carcoon' simply kept the moisture in the air inside the cell and circulated it around the car more efficiently! The rust positively blossomed. It did stop a disintegrating garage roof from damaging the car though, so decide if you really need that level of protection before you make the leap.

5

Where to go for Help

Places to Go – People to See!

Sometimes the most prominent dealers are just that because they charge more than anywhere else. It's not always the cheapest, or the best way to keep your pride and joy in prime condition.

Main dealers have the largest overheads and their contracts with the manufacturer mean they are rarely ever competitive with smaller 'specialists'. The reasonable assumption that the main dealer must know what they are doing better than anyone else is not necessarily as reasonable as you might think. I remember having my Elise at the main dealers for its first service in my ownership, and the first time I had taken a Lotus to the dealers for that type of basic work. After waiting for an hour in the showroom I was invited into the workshop, where the head of the service department was leaning into the engine bay with a puzzled look, cocking his head to the side to listen to the engine more closely.

'It's not idling properly is it?' he ventured. It had a slightly lumpy idle that I had put down to the modifications it was fitted with. He then took one of the electrical connections to the fuel injectors off and leaned in again. 'You see it's running on three cylinders!' he crowed proudly.

'Of course it is, you've got the injector connection in your hand!' I retorted.

He replaced the one he had removed and proceeded to take the next one off. The engine again ran on the three remaining cylinders. 'You see, it's doing it again!'

I looked at a standing mechanic with a look of pure derision. 'If you keep taking the leads off it's going to run on three cylinders! That's because the injector stops working,' I explained, in a voice reminiscent of Del Boy Trotter talking to Rodney.

'Well I don't know what's wrong with it then!' he stropped, and switched the car off.

'That's pretty obvious! There's nothing wrong with it!' was my reply. He agreed and I arranged to have the bill paid and book stamped.

'Oh by the way, it needs new rear discs and pads. They are £850 from Lotus,' was his parting shot.

'In your dreams!' was mine.

Striking turbo in blue!

The discs were fine for two more years' motoring and even then only required a £20 skim and tidy and are still on the car now, some twelve years later!

The Esprit, especially in older, earlier models, is not a complicated car. There is no engine management, no traction control, and not even fuel injection to worry about. The engine is basic and although carburettors are becoming the domain of the wise and the old, they are actually fairly easy to work on, with very few moving parts. Changing cam belts is tricky only in the fact that there is little room to work in.

Later models and 'Turbo' models do become more complicated in the engine bay, but are easily worked on by any competent mechanic.

Information and Clubs

First of all, a cautionary note about Lotus internet forums, as with all websites, social media and forums. There are those among us who have never wielded a spanner in frustration, but who have read all of the books and magazine articles, possibly own the car – even if only in 1:18 scale – and have studied the workshop manual and parts list in minutiae. These are the BBEs, as Mike and I call them – Back Bedroom Experts!

Most decent forums have moderators who remove erroneous and fanciful posts, but I once read that the water seen dripping from the exhaust pipe of an Esprit, just after it had been started and was warming, was the result of a blown cylinder head gasket and would require comprehensive work at a Lotus dealership! You have been warned! The water was obviously condensation in the latter part of the exhaust system, which disappeared when the car was run for a while and had warmed through to the end of the exhaust pipe.

Here is a selection of websites where we trust the content:

Esprit World (http://www.lotusespritworld.com/) – The place for information and advice on the Esprit, in all its model forms. Comprehensive forums and loads of content.
Lotus Excel Net (http://www.lotusexcel.net/phpbb/) – Can help with engine information for earlier normally aspirated Esprits and for supplies of parts, and who originally made them. There are lots of cross-over parts between Excel and Esprit models.
SELOC – South East Lotus Owners' Club (https://www.seloc.org/) – Good site if you prefer a 'club' feel. Events, membership discounts and a free-to-users forum. This site caters for all Lotus models but has interesting information and is particularly useful for later Esprit models.
The Lotus Forums (https://www.thelotusforums.com/) – Another really good site with tons of information and resources.
Parts Manuals & Information (http://www.rdent.com/manuals/index.html) – Parts information and manuals up to the Esprit 2.2 are available on this site. This is really useful if you need instant viewing of a parts manual, or have not gone to the expense of purchasing said manuals!

Mechanicals

QED (Quorn Engine Developments) (http://qedmotorsport.co.uk/) – Lotus experts. They provide next-day delivery and comprehensive expertise and knowledge of all Lotus engines.
Lotus Bits (http://www.lotusbits.com/) – Lotus Bits have been around for a long while and supply very good second-hand and reconditioned parts for all of the modern range of Lotus cars. Good prices and they might have what others don't!
SJ Sportscars (http://www.sjsportscars.co.uk/index.php?mod=9) – Good range of parts and a website that works well – there is generally a photo of the part with a description. Keen enough prices and 'Steve's alternative' parts make this a good place to look.
Kelvedon (http://www.kelsport.net/) – Very knowledgeable and good prices. They prepare Lotuses for racing – say no more!
Eurocarb (http://www.dellorto.co.uk) – All of the parts, jets, trumpets etc. for the Dellorto carburettors on all Lotus models. Usually the best prices as well.

Bodywork

This really is the expert discipline in Lotus terms. Not just any repairer is adept at fibreglass repairs, nor at preparing and painting fibreglass cars. Some regular coachworks won't entertain the idea of working on fibreglass as it produces a huge amount of dust that can contaminate the paint-shop. This is when you need to use a specialist or, alternatively, someone who works with plastic and fibreglass as part of their craft – car customisers, for example. Always ask to see examples of their work; especially examples that have stood the test of time. Expect a reasonable cost with good fibreglass repairs and painting.

Always monitor any paintwork you have had done for a while after the work has been completed. Badly prepared paintwork will develop blisters or blebs, or even small splits in the paint coat. This is because of moisture leeching through the fibreglass from behind and through the badly prepared 'gel-coat' upon which the paint sits.

Dellorto carburettors ready to go back on a turbo engine.

From the business side!

Insurance

Insurance is getting more difficult to find at reasonable cost. The smaller, cheaper, independent insurance specialists have become bigger, greedier concerns over the years, so shop around and compare quotes.

You need to understand that 'classic' policies are slightly different to standard car policies. There are several important facilities in a classic policy that you need to consider. 'Agreed Value' is just what it sounds like; you agree the value of your car at the outset of your policy and, in the unfortunate event of you writing off the vehicle during your ownership, there is no quibbling about how much your settlement will be for your loss.

Limited mileage policies allow you to specify a limit on your annual mileage that reduces the insurer's risk and therefore the premium charged. The least mileage is usually 1,500 miles, rising in 1,500-mile increments to about 5,000 miles at the most. You might find restricting your miles is very beneficial to your budget and 3,000 miles is quite a reasonable allowance on a second, cherished motor that you don't take out in inclement weather.

Some policies allow you the option of buying back your beloved, again in the event of a total insurance write-off. You may want to consider this option seriously, as most of the time what an insurance company considers an 'uneconomic repair' is nothing of the sort if done by specialists rather than main dealers. If you can undertake some of the work yourself you could even end up with a tidy sum left after the repairs, which you can use to run your pride and joy for several more years.

Here is a head start on where to look for your cover:

Classicline (http://www.classiclineinsurance.co.uk/) – By far the cheapest insurance we have found for Lotus cars in general and for a long time. They do multiple car policies as well. Unlimited mileage, breakdown cover, and agreed value on classic policies. Haven't had to claim yet though!

Footman James (http://www.footmanjames.co.uk/) – Used to be the best for Lotus, and might still be where you live. Worth trying, and you can get a quote online.

Adrian Flux (https://www.adrianflux.co.uk/classics/) – Very close on price and certainly plenty of experience in the classics field. Lots of types of insurance too. Give it a go.

Peter Best Insurance (https://www.peterbestinsurance.co.uk/) – Again worth a try but less competitive since it expanded as a company.

Parts and Replacements

Tyres

Demon Tweeks (http://www.demon-tweeks.co.uk/) – Very good for performance tyres and in odd sizes, so a good place to look.

Black Circles – This is another place that stocks almost every size of tyre and is extremely keen on price.

Always check the recommended forums first for where they are currently finding the best tyres at the best prices, as limited runs of specialist tyres can sometimes become available. This is a great source of useful tyre information – http://www.carbibles.com/tyre_bible.html

Carpets

Coverdale (http://www.carcarpets.co.uk/) – Sets for the Esprit start below £200 and go up to nearly twice this price for the woollen 'luxury' range. A great selection of colours to suit any interior. Even the cheapest range on offer is very good quality and fit, and is easily fitted by anyone with the most basic of skills. They even offer contrasting piping on your carpets if you ask nicely!

Leather Care / Restoration

This is an area where you can get staggering results just by taking some time to watch the tutorial videos on how to use their products that Liquid Leather have posted on YouTube, and spending several hours of hard and concentrated work on your interior. Even just using their 'Scuffmaster' product will reinvigorate very tired, creased-looking leather, but their re-colouring products will make your leather look like new from the factory! This really is an area where time and elbow-grease show great rewards, without expert intervention or expense. Have a go! Gliptone – (https://www.liquidleather.com/)

Extras – Some Rare Models and James Bond of Course!

The Riddle of Pre-Production Prototype Essex Turbo Esprit MPW71V (Chassis No. 10860) – Mike's second Esprit!

Back in 1991, having owned my first Lotus – an S2 Esprit – the only way I could afford to own my dream car – a Lotus Turbo Esprit – would have been to have 'won the pools'; there was no National Lottery back then. However, having extensively restored my S2 Esprit, I had developed some contacts close to the Research and Development Engineering Department at Lotus. I was offered the opportunity to buy a factory development Turbo Esprit along with a new HC turbo engine and gearbox, and all the parts required to convert this development car back to standard Turbo Esprit specification; all for the same price I could achieve selling my S2 Esprit. The deal was very quickly done.

I was the proud owner of a Copper Fire Turbo Esprit, registration MPW71V. The registration seemed very familiar, so a quick check of my library of Lotus books produced a picture of MPW71V – not as a copper-coloured car, but as an Essex Blue Commemorative Turbo Esprit. This had me puzzled. However, upon close inspection of MPW71V, I could see that where the paint had been chipped there were a number of layers of paint. The car certainly had been Essex blue; then there was a white layer of paint, and then there was the current top colour of Copper Fire. In fact, looking down the sides of the car – just visible if you knew where to look – were the ghost lines of where the Essex decals had been.

In fact, when I checked the chassis number in my books, 10860 was one of three chassis numbers missing between S2 production ending and S2.2 production starting. With further research, the three cars turned out to all be Essex Turbo Esprit prototypes featured in many books.

This set me thinking – why was this Lotus dev car re-painted after being originally an Essex blue commemorative model; first to white, then to Copper Fire – the same colour as the Esprit used in *For Your Eyes Only*? It occurred to me; could MPW71V be a 'Bond car'? My research continues and will be the subject of future scribbling!

When I first inspected MPW71V, I found the following differences from the subsequent standard-production Turbo Esprit. Technical differences on purchase were:

MPW81V back in the 90s.

Front vented discs.
Larger radiator than normal.
Larger servo for the brakes.
Outboard rear brakes solid discs.
5-stud BBS front wheels.
4-stud Compomotive split-rim rear wheels.
Rear spring ride height increase spacers.
Modified engine mounting points.
Modified, strengthened rear chassis space frame.
A 'bulbous' cover in place of central map pocket.
Heightened rear engine compartment lid and modified tailgate.
Modified lower rear valance with cut outs for four exhaust outlets.
Unique rear upper link suspension only present on very early pre-production cars.
Separate wiring harness for a V8 injection engine with extensive vacuum and temperature monitoring system.

During the process of converting MPW back to standard spec for road use, I was extremely fortunate to visit the 1992 Birmingham Motor Show and have a chance meeting with Patrick Peal on the Lotus Cars stand.

I will never forget the expression on Patrick's face when I produced a photo of MPW71V and asked him if he knew anything of the history of this car. First, he stated I should not have the car as when he last saw MPW, he had instructed for the prototype all-Lotus V8 engine to be removed from the vehicle to prevent the mothballed V8 project leaving the factory intact as a running prototype, as had nearly happened at some point. Patrick then stated that before his current role at Lotus Cars as head of PR he had worked his way up from being a development engineer in the late 70s/early 80s, and as such was very knowledgeable about MPW71V since he had been responsible for MPW during its V8 development work.

We communicated by letter and telephone after the motor show while Patrick refreshed his memory about MPW and consulted with colleagues about the car. MPW71V was confirmed as being quite a significant vehicle within the development of the Esprit and can claim to be a number of firsts for Lotus and the Esprit model, as listed below.

MPW71V is Pre-Production Essex Turbo Esprit No. 3

MPW71V was originally painted Essex Blue with Essex decals and equipped to full Essex Commemorative specification while testing the new dry sump turbo engine, along with two other identical pre-production Essex prototypes. This alone is quite significant, but MPW then went on to the claim further 'firsts'.

It was the first Esprit to be re-painted the new colour Copper Fire as a screen test car to demonstrate to the Bond film producers this new colour and interior trim, as well as to allow them to screen test the colour to ensure it would work well against a snowy backdrop in Cortina. The trim specification then went onto the option list for production Esprits.

It was the first Esprit to have Lotus embossed into the rear bumper to maximise brand exposure during the Bond film. This was then applied to all production Esprit.

It was the first Lotus car of any car type to be powered by an all-Lotus designed and built V8 engine.

The last development use MPW was involved in at Lotus was to act as a Lotus engineering test bed for the induction system for the Corvette LT5 engine, which Lotus were developing for Chevrolet. It is no surprise to find that the LT5 engine is technically and visually very similar to the earlier mothballed all-Lotus 4-litre V8 project.

The Bond Effect!

Every marque of car has its special model; its one off, must-have model. Sometimes the model changes over time, with fashions and technology, sometimes rarity can be a huge influence on desirability, and sometimes it just has absolute star quality. In the case of the Esprit, several of these factors come together in the Bond cars.

It is already well-documented how the S1 Esprit was put in front of the production team for *The Spy Who Loved Me* in 1977 by parking the car outside the production office and waiting for it to be noticed by the producers. The car used in the film is credited to be PPW306R and this Esprit has changed hands over the years at a massive premium due to

Above: A white S1 Esprit identical to the Bond Esprit. There has been a tendency to have S1s repainted in this colour recently! Note the black front spoiler.

Right: Lights up, showing arrangement of front lights that stayed with the Esprit throughout production.

Rear view of first tail lights arrangement.

its appearance in the movie. Two Esprits were actually used in the film, but it has always been Lotus's policy to credit only one car with the film role. The other Esprit was no doubt pressed into service on display duties or, more likely, development work.

The vehicle details for PPW306R are:

Date of First Registration: 3 August 1976
Year of Manufacture: 1976
Cylinder Capacity (cc): 1,973 cc

The Esprit was so successful in the film that it was brought back in turbo form in 1981 in *For Your Eyes Only*. Disappointingly, it only had a minor role in the film; no spectacular car chases this time, just simple sequences – oh, and being destroyed in an explosion! The total time an Esprit is on screen is only a few minutes. There were two Esprits used in the film – one white and one copper metallic. This is where Mike's research started when he bought MPW71V in December 1991.

The white Esprit was supposed to be OPW654W. The details of the car are:

The Bond Esprit Turbo at Hethel, courtesy of Lotus Cars.

Date of First Registration: 5 August 1980
Year of Manufacture: 1980
This car is white in the film.
There is also the bronze Esprit Turbo OPW678W.

Mike acquired the Esprit – chassis number SCCFC20A6AHD10860 – and discovered it had first been registered on 12 May 1980 and retained by the factory. When Mike got the car home he made copious notes about the modifications Lotus had made to the car during their development work and he has included these in this section.

Mike continued to ask questions about the car as he painstakingly returned the car to the road. MPW71V made its bid for stardom in mid to late 1980, when it was re-painted and re-trimmed in the Copper Fire and sand hide trim that it has to this day. Mike was determined to find out if his car had been in the film, but the factory line was that the car had been painted and trimmed to show Cubby Broccoli what the Esprit would look like for the film – particularly for the scenes in Cortina in the snow, where the white Esprit would not provide enough contrast for the film. Mike has a letter from Patrick Peal, Head of Communications, dated 16 June 1993, detailing the use of the car before he bought it and why it was re-trimmed in the Bond livery.

Mike put the Esprit back together with the HC engine and gearbox. He borrowed some working space from another Esprit Turbo owner and enlisted the expertise and help of North East Lotus Owners Club members, when the need arose. I remember being press-ganged into helping with the rewiring needed in the engine bay before the HC engine could be installed. I was inside the engine bay with my circuit tester and paraphernalia, humming away quite engaged in my very small part of the rebuild, when there was the scattering of clawed paws behind me on the concrete and a barking like the hound of the Baskervilles. I turned just in time to see a mountain of furry flesh bounding towards the back of the car like it had just smelt its dinner. I grabbed the tailgate and pulled it down like a closing mousetrap, just in time! My canine nemesis bumped against the rear bumper and circled the car like a finless shark. Despite my calls for help I was like that for twenty minutes, so I know more than most about the engine bay of the Esprit! Thank goodness the Esprit is so low.

Mike has continued to follow his project over the years and is much closer to discovering just what part his old Esprit had with Mr Bond.

Another Rarity – The Active Suspension Esprit Turbo

Lotus Cars are quite unlike any other major sporting car marques in the way they deal with prototypes and development cars. Lots of these cars are sold on from the factory and end up in the possession of enthusiasts. Can you imagine Porsche, Lamborghini or Ferrari doing anything similar? One such car is the development Esprit, used in the development of an active-ride system for racing and road purposes. Years ahead of the field, as ever! Below is an article from Stuart Monument, who purchased the Esprit from the factory:

The Active Suspension development car.

This car may not need any introduction to a Lotus Esprit enthusiast. This one-off Lotus Active Suspension car was developed in the early 80s to support the development in Formula One as well as possible further application to road cars, agricultural, and army vehicles.

The active car started life as the first pre-production Essex Esprit. It was used by the DeLorean Motor Company and possibly by John DeLorean himself. It was originally Essex Blue with red leather. The original pre-production cars were painted Essex Blue colour code A17. However, when the Essex Esprit went into production, Lotus changed the colour of Essex Blue very slightly to colour code A16.

On return of the car to Lotus, the car was seconded to the engineering department where its life started as the development mule for active suspension. At this time the car was then painted black with its gold pin striping and 'Active Suspension' graphics work.

The car turned out to be pretty groundbreaking not only in technological advances but also drive-ability. The car was reported to have cornering speeds 10% quicker than a standard Esprit with no roll into the corners. On a race track this 10% advantage

A very rare and special car!

Worth a look when it hits the exhibition scene.

would have been a prolific advantage. John Miles (Ex-Lotus Formula One driver) even went as far to say that it was an extraordinary piece of engineering, he would rank it in importance alongside the Lotus Type 25 (Lotus's first monocoque-built car) that took Jim Clark to be a World Champion.

The objective of the Active Suspension was to keep the car level regardless of load and to prevent roll and pitch. The car first ran as an active car in March 1982. This was achieved by a clever computer system (for the time) to sense changes in ride attitude which in turn pumped oil to four hydraulic jacks. The oil could be admitted either side of a piston through an electrically operated servo which could open and close hundreds of times a second, although twenty times a second was considered more than enough.

Unfortunately the development of Active suspension system was cancelled with Colin Chapman's death and rule changes in F1. The car was then left in the car park behind hanger four at the Lotus factory for over ten years and destined to be crushed upon request of senior Lotus personnel. Fortunately a long standing Lotus employee moved and hid the car and managed to stop it meeting its end. He did get a 'telling off' for interfering with company property but has saved a piece of unique Lotus history. A senior person within Lotus at the time then went on to spot the car and asked why it was not being displayed. The car was subsequently 'spruced up' up for display at the base of a main stairwell of a new building at Lotus. The engineers changed the fuel lines, added a battery and fuel to find the car started after years of hibernation. Of course this being one of the early cars it is also has a dry sump engine. The car has still only covered just over 7,000 miles from new.

There are numerous motor press articles available about the Active car including a *Top Gear* video presented by John Miles, interviews with Nigel Mansell driving the car, and also pictures of Prince Charles inspecting the car.

The car currently lives not too many miles from the Lotus factory, where it is the aim of the current owner to restore the car to full working order and to display it at numerous different Lotus events around the country. The current owner realises what a significant part of Lotus history this car has and wants the Lotus community to enjoy it with him.

Special thanks to Stuart Monument, the present owner of this car, for his pictures and contribution to this book.

The Last Word!

The Lotus Esprit – a true design icon and a British motoring legend. We hope you find your way to at the very least driving an Esprit and, who knows, perhaps actually owning one. If you do we will no doubt see you at one of the organised shows or on a drive out to the Lakes or the like. Enjoy your mileage!